WASHINGTON, D.C.
THEN & NOW

WASHINGTON, D.C.
THEN & NOW

ALEXANDER D. MITCHELL IV

THUNDER BAY
P·R·E·S·S

San Diego, California

Thunder Bay Press
An imprint of the Advantage Publishers Group
THUNDER BAY 5880 Oberlin Drive, San Diego, CA 92121-4794
P·R·E·S·S www.thunderbaybooks.com

Produced by Salamander Books,
an imprint of Anova Books Company Ltd.,
10 Southcombe Street, London, W14 0RA, United Kingdom

All notations of errors or omissions should be addressed to Thunder Bay Press,
Editorial Department, at the above address. All other correspondence (author
inquiries, permissions) concerning the content of this book should be addressed to
Salamander Books, 10 Southcombe Street, London, W14 0RA, United Kingdom.

ISBN-13: 978-1-59223-832-3
ISBN-10: 1-59223-832-7

The Library of Congress has cataloged the original Thunder Bay edition as follows:

Mitchell, Alexander D.
     Washington then & now / Alexander D. Mitchell.
        p. cm.
     Includes index.
ISBN 1-57145-191-9
     1. Washington (D.C.)--Pictorial works. 2. Washington (D.C.)--History--
Pictorial works. I. Title: Washington then and now. II. Title.

F195 .M58 2000
975.3'0022'2--dc21
                                          00-036410

Printed and bound in China

1 2 3 4 5 11 10 09 08 07

ACKNOWLEDGMENTS

The black and white photography was supplied courtesy of the Prints and Photographs Division of the
Library of Congress, with the following exceptions:
Daguerreotype Collection, Prints and Photographs Division, Library of Congress for page 6;
© S. W. Gerber, Prints and Photographs Division, Library of Congress for page 8 (right);
Theodor Horydczak Collection, Prints and Photographs Division, Library of Congress for page 20;
Historical Society of Washington, D.C., for page 24;
Selected Civil War Photographs, 1861–1865 Collection, Prints and Photographs Division, Library of
Congress for page 26 (inset);
Historic American Buildings Survey Collection, Prints and Photographs Division, Library of Congress for
pages 68 and 114;
© Detroit Photo Co., Prints and Photographs Division, Library of Congress for page 88 (main);
© American Press Association, Prints and Photographs Division, Library of Congress for page 108;
James M. Goode Collection, Prints and Photographs Division, Library of Congress for page 110;
© Bettmann/CORBIS for pages 70 and 138;
Hulton Getty Picture Collection for page 140.

The publisher wishes to thank Simon Clay for taking all the Now photographs for this book,
with the exception of: © CORBIS, page 9 (inset), page 11 (inset), page 53, page 55, page 67, page 69,
page 71, page 73, page 75, page 89, and page 143.

Anova Books is committed to respecting the intellectual property rights of others. We have therefore taken
all reasonable efforts to ensure that the reproduction of all content on these pages is done with the full
consent of copyright owners. If you are aware of any unintentional omissions, please contact the company
directly so that any necessary corrections may be made for future editions.

INTRODUCTION

Of all the major cities in the United States, Washington, D.C., must rate as the most untypical and unusual. It is often regarded as the center of power of the United States, and even Western civilization. It could qualify as the first "planned community" in the country, even if the plans were often disregarded and changed over the years. It merits nomination as the largest "company town," what with the huge numbers of federal employees now working in the city. The city's skyline is distinguished by what it doesn't have—an abundance of skyscrapers rising out of the downtown district. And the District of Columbia is truly "monumental," with a memorial, monument, or grand building seemingly within sight or a stone's throw of any place in town.

The area now known as the District of Columbia had its origins in 1785 when, after years of a nomadic existence, the new government of the thirteen former British colonies voted to set up shop in a permanent "federal town." After much debate over whether to place the city on the Delaware River or the Potomac River, the government decided on the southern option. In 1790 George Washington selected the 100-square-mile diamond of land that would be named after him. It incorporated parts of Alexandria, Virginia (near his own home at Mount Vernon), Georgetown, Maryland, and both banks of the Potomac and Anacostia rivers. The location would be derided in future years as one that was heavy on swamps and mosquitoes, hot and humid in the summer, and cold and icy in the winter.

Pierre Charles L'Enfant, a French engineer and architect who had served with Washington in the Colonial army, offered his services to design a capital city worthy of a great nation and world recognition. No doubt inspired by the grandeur of Versailles and Paris, he and Andrew Ellicott laid out a visionary grid plan heavy with majestic avenues, a central mall, monumental circles, and spectacular public buildings—the basis of Washington's heart today.

L'Enfant's plan quickly outran the young nation's resources and the ability of economic development to match, and it would take until the era after the Civil War for the combination of a thriving economy and expanding government to raise the city from a backwater company town to a metropolis. By 1900, however, unplanned and haphazard development had so ignored L'Enfant's vision that a congressional committee headed by Senator James McMillan was organized to completely revamp and overhaul the future appearance of Washington. The end result of consultations with architects and artists was the Senate Park Commission Report for Washington, popularly referred to as the McMillan Plan, released in 1902, which would affect the appearance of the city for decades, if not forever. Its major effects over the years were to restore and protect the open spaces of the Mall and create other open plazas and

monuments such as the Union Station Plaza, the Lincoln Memorial, and the Arlington Memorial Bridge. It also capped the height of future buildings just as the skyscraper era began, producing the low-slung skyline that distinguishes the city from almost every other American metropolitan area today.

The next major plan for Washington arose from the Public Buildings Commission, created by Congress in 1916 to address the problems of housing an expanding bureaucracy. Their planning culminated in the Public Buildings Act of 1928, which directly resulted in the construction during the Depression-ridden 1930s of the group of massive federal buildings between Pennsylvania Avenue and the Mall now known as the Federal Triangle. It also resulted in the construction of the Supreme Court Building, the House Office Building, and the Jefferson Memorial.

In common with metropolitan areas in the rest of the nation after World War II, Washington shifted from a thriving residential metropolis to a central business city surrounded by suburban bedroom communities. In all this, the downtown shopping district and much of Pennsylvania Avenue, arguably the nation's showcase boulevard, remained neglected. In 1964 the President's Council on Pennsylvania Avenue, appointed by President John F. Kennedy, submitted a report that guided the redesign of the southeastern end of Pennsylvania Avenue and the commercial district to the north between Sixth and Ninth streets. The redevelopment continues to this day.

Today, Washington endures as a thriving American city, although not without the ills affecting many other American cities—crime, suburbanization, and traffic congestion—and troubles unique to the District of Columbia, including endless political wrangling. As the twenty-first century approached, the district struggled to get aboard the economic boom that had swept the United States after the Cold War, and struggled anew to gain political autonomy in the form of home rule or statehood.

This book, just like the photographs inside, cannot be a definitive interpretation or history of the city. Rather, it is a moment frozen in time, sometimes perilously. For every scene in the book that is seemingly preserved for the ages by planning and legislation, there is another where construction cranes hover and buildings are rising or falling as these words are written. For every scene that would take no effort for the first-time visitor to find, there were scenes that led to enormous perplexity and searching. Jonathan Swift noted that "there is nothing in this world constant, but inconstancy," and that is particularly apt in the case of photographic histories. With that, I hope that you enjoy the small slice of the District of Columbia's historic panorama that I was able to bring you, and hope that readers in the future can also partake in the sense of discovery and exploration that we enjoyed while producing this book.

The earliest known photograph of the Capitol, this 1846 daguerreotype is one of a series taken of Washington subjects by John Plumbe Jr., regarded by many as the first professional photographer in the country. Seven are known to survive, including this one, which was among a set purchased at a flea market in Alameda, California, in 1971 for only a few dollars and subsequently sold to the Library of Congress. The old Senate wing, begun in 1793 and completed in 1800, is to the right; the House wing is to the left. Both were torched by British troops in August 1814 during the War of 1812. After rebuilding the fire-devastated wings, Charles Bulfinch began work on the center section in 1818, and completed it in 1829.

In 1850, Congress (which had grown along with the nation) authorized a badly needed expansion of the Capitol, begun the following year. Subsequently, in 1855, Congress authorized a larger dome in keeping with the larger building. Abraham Lincoln performed an inauguration ceremony on March 4, 1861, though the dome was still under construction. Thomas U. Walter was responsible for designing the "wedding cake" cast-iron structure, and drew on the classical domes of Europe for his inspiration. It was three times the height of the original dome and 100 feet in diameter. The above photograph dates to June 1863; when the dome was finally completed by Walter's assistant, Edward Park, in 1868, it was significantly larger than the original plan.

Five "newsies" line up below the steps of the West Front of the Capitol on April 12, 1912. When asked by the photographer how much money he'd made that day, one of the boys replied, "Eight cents." Being truant from school was not uncommon in the early twentieth century and, despite its status as the nation's seat of government, Washington has always had a large population of those affected by poverty. Four days later, these boys are likely to have sold every newspaper they possessed as news of the *Titanic*'s sinking hit the front pages.

In the twenty-first century, news is still made on Capitol Hill but not sold on the steps of the West Front. Since the introduction of electric floodlighting, the seat of the nation's government has been bathed nightly in a spectacular blaze of glory, save for wartime blackouts. The modern photo of the East Front (right) shows what appears to be the same portico and walls, but actually shows a new extension built between 1959 and 1961, thirty-four feet out from the old one and which added a hundred additional offices. The stone used for the extension was Georgia marble, not the original sandstone. When further plans were submitted to enlarge the West Front in the 1970s, public protests were sufficient to have them shelved.

Looking northeast on Maryland Avenue, this view from around 1891 shows the completed Capitol, as well as three horse-drawn streetcars. Horse-drawn streetcars began operation in Washington in 1862. The first electric streetcars in the city began operation in 1880, but overhead wires were banned by Congress soon afterward. It took several years for an effective underground conduit system to be developed, a system that gave the tracks the appearance of a cable car system like that of San Francisco.

The last D.C. Transit streetcars operated in January 1962; the Washington Metro subway system was begun in 1969 and opened in 1976. The modern view shows that little has altered other than a change in streetlight hardware and a reduction in foliage. The nineteen-foot bronze statue atop the Capitol dome, *Freedom*, sculpted by Thomas Crawford, was removed from its perch by helicopter for a much-needed cleaning in 1993. The inset photo shows the building's location as it looks west down the National Mall.

French sculptor Frédéric Auguste Bartholdi produced many of the world's most renowned sculptures, including what is arguably the most famous of all, *Liberty Enlightening the World*, more popularly known as the Statue of Liberty in New York Harbor. This fountain, humble by comparison, was built for the Centennial Exhibition in Philadelphia in 1876 and was purchased by the U.S. government in 1877. The inset photo is from the winter of 1901, when the fountain froze.

Originally installed in the Botanic Garden across the street from the Capitol, the Bartholdi Fountain was moved in 1932 to a small triangle west of the Rayburn House Office Building and above Washington Avenue, which is now effectively the end of a major exit ramp from the Southwest/Southeast Freeway (I-395). Thousands of drivers struggle past this fountain daily, perhaps never realizing its significance.

The view east from the Capitol dome in about 1880 depicts the largely residential neighborhood now referred to as Capitol Hill. The massive, twenty-ton marble statue of George Washington in the foreground, done by Horatio Greenough, was commissioned by Congress in 1832 and delivered in 1841. It proved to be too heavy for the Rotunda yet, oddly, too small for the interior, and it spent the next century being moved about the East Grounds and the city like a hapless chess pawn before taking up residence in the Smithsonian's Museum of History and Technology in 1962. At the right center can be seen Carroll Row, the future site of the Library of Congress. Large numbers of newer Victorian homes can also be seen, as can the results of general public works and street regrading—many older buildings are now high above the streets, requiring long stair climbs to the front doors.

The modern view shows foliage obscuring much of what appears in the old photograph, but to the left can be seen the Supreme Court Building and to the right, beyond the trees, the Library of Congress. Note also the concessions to modern security—a heavy police presence and "decorative" planters that actually serve as barricades. Tripods, a necessity in early photography, are no longer allowed on the Capitol grounds without permits.

Built in 1805 by Daniel Carroll, this row of houses across the street from the Capitol grounds was leased to local innkeeper Pontius D. Stelle, who rented rooms to the earliest members of Congress and their visitors and business associates. During the Civil War, it was used to house political prisoners.

The row of houses was demolished in 1886–87 to make way for the Jefferson Building of the Library of Congress, which can be seen on the left. Behind and to the south of the Jefferson Building across Independence Avenue is the newer Madison Building of the Library of Congress, which opened in 1980.

The Library of Congress began as a legislative library in 1800 with the acquisition of 740 books from London, but was destroyed when the British burned Washington in 1814. Thomas Jefferson then sold his 6,437-volume personal library to the government for $23,950 to form the nucleus for a new library. Since then, the Library of Congress has become the de facto national library of virtually all published works in the United States. A more modern library building, now known as the Jefferson Building, was planned in 1871; construction began in 1886 and was completed in 1897. This photograph was taken in 1921.

The Jefferson Building, built in the Italian Renaissance style, was originally planned to house 3 million volumes; the Library of Congress now houses over 100 million items and employs nearly 5,000 people in three adjoining buildings (Jefferson, Adams, and Madison) and off-site storage centers. The inset photos show the Main Reading Room, an awe-inspiring room described as being like the interior of a giant Fabergé egg. Only the glow of laptop computers marks the difference of years in the octagonal mahogany-trimmed shrine to research.

The gem of the Jefferson Building of the Library of Congress, and arguably the whole of Washington, is its spectacular, richly decorated Great Hall. In spite of its outlandish decoration, the building was completed for $200,000 less than the original Congressional authorization of $6.5 million. Of that, $364,000 was used for the costs of painting, sculpture, decoration, and three massive bronze doors.

After eleven years of renovations to its curving marble staircases, bronze statuary, rich mosaics, and paintings and murals that would be the envy of ancient Egypt or Greece, the Jefferson Building was reopened to the public in 1997, the building's centennial year, and today it is as impressive as it was when it was opened— a superb and painstaking job of restoration.

Opened in 1932 and located just down Capitol Street from the Library of Congress (but an independent concern), the Folger Shakespeare Library was a gift to the American people from Henry Clay Folger and his wife, Emily Jordan Folger. The marble Art Deco building was designed by architect Paul Philippe Cret.

A major center for research, the Folger houses the world's largest collection of Shakespeare's printed works in addition to a large collection of other rare Renaissance books and manuscripts on disciplines such as history, theology, politics, and the arts. The collection consists of approximately 280,000 books and manuscripts; 27,000 paintings, drawings, engravings, and prints; and musical instruments, costumes, and films. Also inside is a reproduction of an inn-yard theater, used for theatrical and musical performances.

This location east of the Capitol between East Capitol Street and Maryland Avenue was the site of the "Old Brick Capitol," hastily erected to temporarily replace the burned Capitol in 1814 and used as such until 1819. The building later served as a boardinghouse and school until the government turned it into a Civil War prison, as shown in the inset picture. It was demolished in 1867 and replaced by a row of brick houses, which were soon demolished to make way for the Supreme Court Building. The 1935 view shows the building, designed by Cass Gilbert, at its completion.

The Supreme Court, long without its own home, finally acquired one in 1928 when Congress passed the Public Buildings Act, which, among other things, provided for the construction of the Supreme Court Building. Today the building is the symbol of the federal government's judiciary branch, as it is featured regularly in newscasts and photos, and is also the scene of frequent demonstrations for or against Supreme Court decisions large and small.

The Baltimore & Ohio Railroad was the first intercity railroad in the United States, and its first terminal in the nation's capital was built a block south of this site in 1835, just a few blocks from Capitol Hill. This Italianate-style station, with its tracks primarily below street level, was built at C Street and New Jersey Avenue in 1850–51. The above photograph was taken around 1880. Connections to the South were originally provided with tracks down First Street and Maryland Avenue to the Long Bridge across the Potomac.

Originally seeing a modest three or four trains a day, the depot swiftly became outmoded in the later part of the century, and was demolished in 1907 when it was replaced by the newly built Union Station to the north. The area between Union Station and the Capitol became part of Union Station Plaza under the Public Buildings Act of 1928, and the area is now open green space.

The Government Printing Office (GPO) was created in 1852 to satisfy the printing needs of Congress. Authorized by Congress in 1860, it serves today as the publishing arm of the U.S. government, performing nearly all printing and binding for the entire federal community. It is still regarded as the largest printing plant in the world. This photograph was taken in 1908.

The large redbrick building that houses the GPO was erected in
1903 on G and Capitol streets, and is unusual in being one of the few
large, redbrick government structures in a city that now seems to be
mostly marble and granite. (The Smithsonian Castle and the Pension
Building, now the National Building Museum, are other exceptions.)
An additional structure was attached to its north in later years.

The District of Columbia Fire Department, started as a consolidation of volunteer fire departments in 1864, became fully professional under the DCFD banner in 1871. The last horse-drawn apparatus was retired in 1925. Engine Company 3 occupied this firehouse at C Street and Delaware Avenue, NE, between the Capitol and what became Union Station, in May 1875.

In 1916, Engine Company 3 was moved to 439 New Jersey Avenue, NW, just around the corner; that firehouse was closed in 1993. The 1928 Public Buildings Act that eliminated most structures between Union Station and the Capitol also eliminated this firehouse, and today the location looks at an entrance to the underground parking garage of the Russell Senate Office Building.

At Fourth and D streets, NW, the old city hall, designed by British architect George Hadfield, was begun in 1820 but was completed in 1853 without the planned central dome. A lottery plan failed to raise enough capital to finish the structure, and the federal government allocated funds for its completion on the condition that it be permitted to occupy one wing when it was finished, which it used for circuit and criminal courts.

The district offices were moved in 1908 to the District Building, at Fourteenth Street and Pennsylvania Avenue, NW, and the old city hall stands today in the heart of Judiciary Square; it is still used by the government of the District of Columbia and the U.S. Circuit Court.

The avenue between the White House and Capitol has hosted triumphant and somber parades over the years. (Shown here is the funeral parade for the victims of the 1898 USS *Maine* explosion, also seen on page 134.) The massive edifice in the center of both of these photographs is the Main Post Office, now the third-tallest building in Washington (including the Washington Monument) at 315 feet. Rising to the right is the clock tower of the Southern Railway Building, which was completed in 1903 but destroyed by fire in 1916, four years after this photograph was taken.

The classic view of Washington's grand avenue between the Capitol and the White House is still obtained from the steps of the Treasury Building at Fifteenth Street. The modern view shows the Willard Hotel on the left, with Freedom Plaza (formerly the Western Plaza) disrupting the grand avenue view in the foreground and the Federal Triangle lining almost the whole of the right side of Pennsylvania Avenue.

This overall view of Pennsylvania Avenue depicts pedestrian traffic that would be almost unthinkable today. Note the white-coated street-sweeper to the left. The twin-towered building to the right of center was known as the Central National Bank Building and was erected in 1888. Another bank was established in the building to its left in 1889; just down Pennsylvania Avenue from this structure sits the studio building of early photographer Matthew Brady, now legendary for his Civil War photography.

To the left in the modern photograph is the granite and bronze monument to the Grand Army of the Republic's founder, Dr. Benjamin F. Stephenson, erected in 1909 by the Grand Army and which sits on what is now Indiana Plaza. The twin-towered building is now used by the National Council of Negro Women; the other bank building houses the Riggs National Bank.

This eight-foot marble statue, portraying Benjamin Franklin in the diplomatic dress of American minister to the French government, was donated in 1889 by Stilson Hutchins, the founder of the *Washington Post* and other American newspapers. By 1889 he had sold the *Post*, but he nonetheless donated the statue to honor one of America's first journalists and printers of note. To the right in the photo is an office of the *Post*, which had moved from its old home at Tenth and D streets (now covered by the FBI Building).

The humble statue to Benjamin Franklin, a Founding Father of the country, has seen nearly everything around it change. Behind the statue in the modern photo is a corner of the Old Post Office, and to the right rear are buildings occupied by the Interstate Commerce Commission.

The building now known as the Old Post Office was built in 1899 to serve as the main city post office (until 1914, when it was replaced by a new post office across the street from Union Station) and as offices of the U.S. Post Office Department (until 1934). Noted for its 315-foot clock tower (the third-tallest landmark in Washington) and its elaborate Flag Day pageantry and displays, it was the first federal building along Pennsylvania Avenue between the White House and the Capitol, and the first in what would eventually become known as the Federal Triangle. This photo shows a Flag Day display circa 1910.

The Old Post Office would be the only building in the Federal Triangle to survive the reconstruction of neoclassical federal buildings throughout the area. After the building endured numerous occupants and threats of demolition, preservationists were successful in saving the building, and it was renovated from 1978 to 1983 for commercial and office use. It now houses the National Endowment for the Humanities and a shopping court.

This view from about 1890 shows the haphazard architecture typical of the post–Civil War Pennsylvania Avenue on a section that housed a great many newspaper offices. Prominent on the near corner is the office of the *Washington Evening Star*, which was founded in 1852 and occupied a building on the southwest corner of this intersection from 1854 to 1881. The newspaper then moved around this side of Pennsylvania Avenue to utilize various buildings until 1898, when it moved into the building that now stands on this corner.

The *Evening Star* outlived a hundred other newspapers in the city but finally folded in 1981, a victim of declining evening newspaper circulation nationwide. The building at 1101 Pennsylvania Avenue continues to be known as the Evening Star Building, even though it now houses offices and has added its next-door neighbor. On the Eleventh Street side is the entrance to a Planet Hollywood restaurant; while its neighbor at 1111 Pennsylvania Avenue comprises office suites. This area of town is favored by major law firms, government agencies, and lobbyist groups.

Central Market was the largest of five major markets in the city (of which only Eastern Market, at Seventh Street and South Carolina Avenue, SE, survives today) and among the largest market houses in the nation, offering space for up to 300 vendors and their wagons.

Designed by Adolph Cluss and built in 1871–73 on the site of the city's earliest primary market, it was conveniently located on the Washington Canal (now Constitution Avenue), which allowed for the daily delivery of fresh produce.

The Central Market had lost much of its business to corner stores
and supermarkets when it was demolished in 1931 as part of the
Federal Triangle redevelopment project. The National Archives was
built on the site in 1931–34; it houses the original Declaration of
Independence, the United States Constitution, and the Bill of Rights.

This photograph depicts a meeting of the National Equal Rights Convention at the Metzerott Hotel at 925 Pennsylvania Avenue in Washington, D.C., on December 9, 1873. Regrettably, no other information could be found about this meeting; the National Association for the Advancement of Colored People, now the largest and most significant civil-rights group in America, was not founded until 1910.

At the location today is the much-maligned J. Edgar Hoover Building of the Federal Bureau of Investigation, opened in 1974 with a design (frequently referred to sarcastically as "neo-Brutalism") that is quite inconsistent with the Federal Triangle district across the street. The building's erection at the site may be regarded as considerably ironic, given Hoover's record (or lack thereof) on civil rights during the 1960s.

Originally founded as the City Hotel in 1816 by Benjamin Ogle Tayloe, the hotel would later be named after Henry Willard, who took over the hotel in the 1850s. Due to its central location at Fourteenth Street and Pennsylvania Avenue, NW, and its proximity to the White House, it became a center of political and social activity for decades. Among the famous short-term occupants were Charles Dickens (in 1842) and presidents Taylor, Fillmore, Buchanan, and Lincoln. In 1861, Julia Ward Howe wrote "The Battle Hymn of the Republic" while staying at the hotel. The term "lobbyist" was supposedly coined by President Grant to refer to power brokers that continually courted him in the Willard's lobby. The old building in the front of the photograph was expanded with newly built sections uphill and to the right in 1858.

The current building was constructed here in 1901 (see inset opposite) and was designed by Henry Hardenbergh, who also designed New York's Plaza and Waldorf-Astoria hotels. Martin Luther King Jr. wrote his epic "I have a dream" speech here before delivering it at the Lincoln Memorial in August 1963. The hotel fell upon hard times after World War II, closing in 1968 and remaining empty until 1986, when it reopened after an extensive renovation; it remains an active hotel today.

The Ebbitt House Hotel on the southeast corner of Fourteenth and F streets (across the street from the Willard) distinguished itself by being the first hotel in Washington to remain open all summer instead of closing when Congress adjourned. It was demolished in 1925, and the National Press Building was erected on the site in 1926. The latter fell upon hard times during the Great Depression but rebounded after World War II, becoming host to offices, shops, and a theater.

The building was reconstructed beginning in 1982, a popular shopping mall was added, but the original facade was altered. World leaders and dignitaries, from Churchill to Gandhi to Lindbergh to various presidents, have visited the Press Club that occupies the top floor.

The building also covers the site (1336–38 F Street) of the Washington home of Aaron Burr, Jefferson's vice president, who killed Alexander Hamilton in a duel in 1804.

Located at the most famous address in the nation, 1600 Pennsylvania Avenue, the oldest public building in Washington at first looks little changed from its original design by James Hoban, which was based on country estate houses in Britain and Ireland. However, many changes have occurred. Construction began in 1793 and was complete enough for John Adams to move in at the end of his term in 1800. It was rebuilt under Hoban's supervision between 1815 and 1817 after its torching by the British in 1814. It was officially known as the Executive Mansion for its first century.

Over the years, successive occupants of the White House have made additions and refurnishings as progress allowed, including gas lighting (seen in the old view of the north portico), central heating, plumbing, and electricity. President Theodore Roosevelt officially changed the name of the residence to the White House in 1901 and undertook a major reconstruction of the interior in 1902. Also changed frequently was the landscaping surrounding the building, as seen in these two views of the North Lawn.

During World War I, a herd of sheep was permitted to live on the White House's South Lawn, ostensibly for propaganda as much as the contribution they made to the war-thinned wool supplies. More significant modifications continued on the building over the years, including the addition of the Rose Garden in 1913, a third floor for more living space (mostly hidden behind the rooftop railings) in 1927, and the East Wing in 1942.

A 1948 examination under the Truman administration revealed such severe deterioration that Truman moved across the street to the Blair House while a complete interior reconstruction was undertaken, with steel and concrete replacing wood and masonry. The balcony seen on the south portico was also added at the time. Today the White House enters its third century as the symbol of the executive branch of the United States government, and more redecorating occurs with each successive occupant.

The Octagon House, also known as the Dolley Madison House, was designed by William Thornton and built by John Tayloe III in 1799 for the princely sum of $26,000—twice the estimates. The house, at 1741 New York Avenue, NW, became the temporary residence of James and Dolley Madison after the burning of the White House by the British in August 1814. The Treaty of Ghent, which ended the war with Britain and formed the basis of British-American relations for the next two centuries, was signed in the main parlor room above the entrance on February 17, 1815. This photograph dates from 1913.

The Octagon House became the home of the American Institute of Architects in 1899. In 1965, the AIA sold the Octagon to its nonprofit arm, now known as the American Architectural Foundation, which operates a museum in the building. The building to the rear, opened in 1973, now holds the expanded offices of the AIA.

The headquarters of the Pan American Union, later the Organization of American States, was built at Seventeenth Street and Constitution Avenue, NW, on the site of the Burnes House, one of the earliest houses in what would become the District of Columbia. Located adjacent to the White House's South Lawn and at the very geographical center of the district, the Burnes House was built around 1750 by David Burnes, who died in 1799 after marketing many parcels of land in the immediate vicinity. An attempt at preservation was made by his sole daughter and her husband, who had built the adjacent Van Ness Mansion in 1816, but the Burnes House was demolished in 1894.

The property was sold to the government in 1907 after being used for everything from a beer garden to an athletic club to a street cleaners' headquarters. Andrew Carnegie donated $900,000 of the $1.1 million cost of the new building. The Pan American Union, formed in 1890, became the Organization of American States in 1948. It is a regional coalition consisting primarily of Latin American and Caribbean nations, generally diplomatic and ceremonial in function, that works with the United Nations.

The old Department of State, War, and Navy Building (later known as the Old Executive Office Building), arguably the most grandiose and ostentatious building in Washington, sits to the immediate west of the White House. Commissioned by Ulysses S. Grant and built between 1871 and 1888 on the site of the original 1800 State, War, and Navy Building and the White House stables, this massive structure was for years the world's largest office building, with 566 rooms and about ten acres of floor space. This photograph was taken in 1908.

Patterned after French Second Empire architecture that clashed sharply with the neoclassical style of other federal buildings in the city, it was generally regarded with scorn and disdain, and the architect of the exterior, Alfred B. Mullett, ended his life in litigation and suicide. The building is now popular with occupants, many of whom come from the executive branch of the government; Vice President Dan Quayle maintained his office here. To this day, it is said to be the largest granite structure of any kind in the world.

Unbelievably, this homely little house that sits at Constitution Avenue and Seventeenth Street near the White House, looking for all the world like a grandiose public toilet, is one of the oldest surviving houses in Washington. Even more incredible, it guarded the junction of what were once the major national transportation arteries—the Potomac River and the Washington branch of the Chesapeake and Ohio Canal. Erected around 1835, it housed the keeper of the canal lock between the Washington Canal and the Chesapeake and Ohio branch, and sat on a narrow spit of land between the canal and the river. Landfill would later place this structure blocks from the Tidal Basin and nearly a half-mile from the Potomac proper.

As the canal's use ended in the 1870s, the building served a variety of ignominious roles, including housing for squatters (as in the vintage photograph, which was taken in 1895). Today it sits empty but is preserved by the National Park Service, occupying a corner opposite from one of Charles Bulfinch's guardhouses for the White House.

This grandiose art gallery at Seventeenth Street and Pennsylvania Avenue was given to the city by philanthropist William Wilson Corcoran, a member of the Corcoran and Riggs firm that eventually grew into the local Riggs National Bank chain. Designed by James Renwick Jr., construction on the building began in 1859, five years after Corcoran's retirement, and was completed as the Corcoran Gallery in 1871. The unfinished building was seized by the U.S. government for office space during the Civil War; Corcoran's board of trustees sued for back rent and eventually collected $125,000.

The Corcoran Gallery was moved in 1897 to a new building at Seventeenth Street and New York Avenue, NW. The original gallery, now known as the Renwick Gallery and part of the Smithsonian's extensive complex, is used to display exhibitions of American craft art. The Grand Salon inside has been restored in the style of the late nineteenth century.

Construction on the memorial to the nation's first president was begun in 1848, but funding by public contribution ran out in 1853; it stood uncompleted at 152 feet for nearly twenty-five years. The federal government later approved funds to complete the structure and it was finished in December 1884 to a design radically simplified from Robert Mills's original colonnaded temple. Close examination will reveal a slight change in the stone color at the 152-foot level, where Massachusetts marble was substituted for the earlier Maryland marble. The smaller photograph above shows a cleaning project in 1934–35, which took a matter of weeks.

The end of the twentieth century brought a dramatic change to one of the most recognizable monuments in the world as scaffolding and shrouding was erected for cleaning and repairing the 555-foot structure. The shrouding of the monument for over a year was originally greeted with aversion, but ironically, as the scaffolding was being disassembled in 2000, efforts were being made to preserve and reerect the scaffolding and its sympathetic shrouding elsewhere. The restoration process involved the sealing of 500 feet of exterior and interior stone cracks and the pointing of 64,000 linear feet of exterior joints.

The marshy ground between the Lincoln Memorial and the Washington Monument was extensively excavated by the Corps of Engineers in the years following World War I to create the Reflecting Pool. The ground between the Lincoln Memorial and the Capitol Building was notoriously difficult to build on. Congress gave Lieutenant Colonel Thomas Casey the responsibility for completing the Washington Monument between 1876 and 1844 after a private organization ran out of money. The Reflecting Pool is built on a continuous membrane.

The National World War II Memorial is dedicated to the 16 million Americans who served in the armed forces during World War II, the more than 400,000 who died, and the millions who contributed to the war effort. Located on the axis of the National Mall, it lies between the Washington Monument and the Lincoln Memorial. It was dedicated by President George W. Bush on May 29, 2004. Friedrich St. Florian's design won the competition set in motion by President Bill Clinton and administrated by the American Battle Monument's Commission. The monument is said to balance classical and modernist styles of architecture and connect the legacy of the American Revolution and the Civil War with the great crusade to rid the world of fascism. Senator Bob Dole, twice a recipient of the Bronze Star, and Frederick W. Smith, a former Marine officer and the CEO of FedEx Corporation, helped raise $197 million for the project.

The year is 1927 and the girls' rifle association of George Washington University poses on the grass of what will become Constitution Gardens, just off Henry Bacon Drive, NW. Much of the land was taken over by the Navy during World War I, and "temporary" offices were erected on the location. President Richard Nixon, who had served in Washington during his time as a naval officer, got the offices demolished in 1971, and a park was built on the site. The park was opened in 1976 as part of the bicentennial celebrations.

In 1984 a monument was dedicated to the American men and women who had fought in Vietnam. Known officially as the Vietnam Veterans Memorial and unofficially as "VVM" or simply "the Wall," it was designed by Maya Ying Lin, who submitted her winning design to a national design competition in 1981. The monument consists of three elements: the wall with inscribed names of casualties from the theaters of Vietnam, Laos, and Cambodia; a statue (inset); and a flagpole. In 2007 there were 58,256 names on the wall; each year, a few more names of servicemen who died due to war-related injuries are added.

The Lincoln Memorial was constructed between 1914 and 1921 to a design (modeled after a Greek temple) by Henry Bacon and was dedicated in 1922. The memorial has thirty-six Doric columns, representing the states of the union at the time of Lincoln's death, and is centered by the famous heroic statue of Lincoln by Daniel Chester French. Frequent icy winters made the Reflecting Pool a popular place for ice-skating, and it was not uncommon to see children riding sleds down the snow-covered steps.

This photograph shows the dramatic lighting employed to highlight Lincoln's statue as he looks out in stern contemplation over the Refelecting Pool toward Capitol Hill. The 2,000-foot-long Reflecting Pool was inspired by similar pools at the Taj Mahal and Versailles. Henry Bacon's name was given to the road running northwest from in front of the memorial through Constitution Gardens.

The memorial to Thomas Jefferson on the Tidal Basin was authorized by Congress, built from 1938 to 1942, and dedicated in 1943. Designed by John Russell Pope (who also did the National Gallery of Art and the National Archives), the white marble structure features a nineteen-foot-tall bronze statue of the third president, sculpted Rudolph Evans, surrounded by twenty-six columns.

The Tidal Basin, upon which the memorial sits, was created in 1882
to trap overflow water from the Potomac River and drain it into the
Washington Channel. It is ringed with cherry trees given by the city
of Tokyo to the city of Washington. The first shipment arrived in 1912.
The annual springtime blooming of these trees is now an internationally
renowned tourist attraction.

The seven buildings that occupy the north side of the 2000 block of Pennsylvania Avenue, NW, were built around 1800 by Isaac Pollock, an important early investor in the city who—like many early investors—lost almost all his money on property ventures gone sour. For a period, the buildings housed the U.S. Department of State.

Only one of the buildings, privately owned and actually a consolidation of parts of two of the older buildings, survives today, sandwiched between the Hotel Lombardi and a newer brick residence and office building.

This photo shows what was once the transportation hub of Washington, the Baltimore & Potomac Railroad Station at Sixth Street and B Street (now Constitution Avenue). Built in 1873 as the Washington terminal for what would become part of the Pennsylvania Railroad's vast network, its departure tracks stretched south across the Mall parallel to Sixth Street. The station secured its notorious place in the history books on July 2, 1881, when President James Garfield was shot in a waiting room by Charles Guiteau, a disgruntled and deranged lawyer who had come to Washington seeking a job appointment. Garfield died two months later.

The station was replaced by Union Station in 1907 and subsequently demolished as part of the McMillan Plan. The site now houses the west wing of the Smithsonian's National Gallery of Art, built in 1941 to a design by John Russell Pope, who also designed the very similar-looking Jefferson Memorial but died in 1937, before either was completed.

In perhaps the sharpest contrast in this book, railroad workers can be
seen clearing snow from the tracks leading to the train shed of the
Baltimore & Potomac Railroad Station after the blizzard of 1893.
This picture was taken from a bridge over the tracks in the vicinity of
present-day Independence Avenue.

The modern view looks out the main exhibition hall of the
Smithsonian's National Air and Space Museum, which opened in
1976. The National Gallery of Art can be seen across a now-open
Mall, underneath the wing of Charles Lindbergh's *Spirit of St. Louis*,
and over a Wright brothers plane.

In this view from around 1880, a class D 4-4-0 locomotive of the Pennsylvania Railroad crosses Maryland Avenue between Sixth and Seventh streets on its final approach to the Baltimore & Potomac depot. Not only did Pennsylvania Railroad trains cross the heart of the Mall until 1907, but Maryland Avenue was once the route for much of the nation's rail traffic between the North and the South before and after the Civil War. Note the gas lamps and the long crossing gates.

The modern view through a realigned intersection is partially blocked by the south wall of the National Air and Space Museum to the left. The Department of Health and Human Services and the Rayburn Office Building of the House of Representatives can be seen further up Independence Avenue.

Washington Union Terminal was begun in 1903 and opened in October 1907 as a joint station of the Pennsylvania Railroad, the Baltimore & Ohio Railroad, and other tenant railroads at the junction of Massachusetts and Delaware avenues. Designed by Daniel H. Burnham, the massive Roman Beaux Arts marble and granite building is marginally larger than the Capitol itself, and includes a concourse measuring 760 feet by 130 feet, said to be the largest room of any kind in the world when it was built.

The station fell into disuse as the importance of passenger trains declined after World War II, and it fell victim to an abortive attempt to build a national visitors' center for the bicentennial in 1976. In the 1980s, however, the station was turned over to the Federal Department of Transportation and dramatically redeveloped into a combined passenger terminal and commercial retail center, with enormous success. It now rivals the National Air and Space Museum as the most-visited Washington attraction. The rail station still sees an average of nearly 100 trains per day.

The Smithsonian Institution was founded in 1846 with $550,000 bequeathed to the United States by English scientist James Smithson "for the increase and diffusion of knowledge." The first of what would become over a dozen Smithsonian buildings scattered across the Mall and Washington, the red sandstone "Castle" was designed by James Renwick Jr. (who also designed New York's St. Patrick's Cathedral) and was completed in 1855. This photo from an early stereopticon card dates to approximately 1880.

The Smithsonian Institution has evolved into the world's largest museum complex and the official repository of American artifacts. The Castle houses the Smithsonian Information Center and many of the institution's administrative offices, as well as the tomb of Smithson.

The General Post Office, the U.S. Patent Office, and the U.S. Treasury were all principally designed (in part, as permanent fireproof buildings) by Robert Mills, who was appointed as the federal architect of public buildings by President Andrew Jackson in 1836. That same year, construction began on the Treasury Building on a site personally selected by Jackson. It was the first radical departure from the city plan drafted by L'Enfant. The building features seventy-four granite columns, all shipped in from Maine quarries.

The southern facade features a statue of Alexander Hamilton, the first
Treasury secretary. Featured on the back of every $10 bill, the building
continues to house the Treasury Department. The original sandstone
colonnades, however, were replaced with granite in 1907.

The National Archives is the official depository for records and documents of the federal government. In 1926, after decades of records being lost to haphazard accounting and storage, Congress arranged for the construction of a space where records could be assembled, stored, and preserved. In 1934 the National Archives was organized, to be administered by a central archivist, and the building was completed on the site of the former Central Market.

The National Archives is perhaps best known among tourists as the building that houses the original copies of the Declaration of Independence, the United States Constitution, and the Bill of Rights. Like many buildings housing federal agencies in Washington, the National Archives' duties are now supplemented by additional facilities in suburban Maryland.

The U.S. Patent Office is the country's headquarters of invention registration. Construction began in 1836 and was completed in 1867. During the Civil War, the uncompleted building was used as a hospital. Burned in 1877, it was rebuilt in the 1880s by noted architect Adolph Cluss. After its renovation, part of the building housed a small museum of patent models of many important American inventions. The actual offices of the U.S. Patent Office were moved in 1932, and the building was then occupied by the Civil Service Commission until 1952.

Slated for demolition, the U.S. Patent Office was spared primarily
through the efforts of David Finley, the chairman of the Fine Arts
Commission, and was transferred to the Smithsonian Institution. It
was restored in 1968 as the headquarters of the National Museum of
American Art and the National Portrait Gallery.

This 1920s view shows one part of the heart of the downtown shopping district at Pennsylvania Avenue and Seventh Street. S. Kann Sons department store was located in the building that originally housed the first clothing store operated by Isidore and Andrew Saks (of Saks Fifth Avenue fame), which later became the Boston Dry Goods store, which itself grew into the local Woodward & Lothrop chain.

Kann's occupied the building from 1886 until the building's demolition in 1979 following a serious fire. The site is now the location of the U.S. Navy Memorial, dedicated in October 1987, which includes an amphitheater for performances by the Navy band and other groups.

This view looking west from the steps of the U.S. Patent Office, taken around 1900, shows a rapidly developing commercial district downtown. To the left is the Washington Loan & Trust Co. Building, erected in 1890, and later the Riggs National Bank WL&T branch.

Behind the bank is the recently built National Union Insurance Company Building, with its sign at the top plainly visible. To the right at 901 F Street is the Masonic Temple, begun in 1868, which had shops on the ground floor and meeting rooms above.

In the modern view, a hotel chain occupies the former WL&T
building; the signage for the insurance company is still faintly
visible, and the Masonic Temple, vacant for over twenty years,
was redeveloped as commercial space as the Gallup Building. The
Treasury Building can be seen at the far end of F Street in both views.

Left: This was the home of Salmon P. Chase, one of the lesser-known but still important figures in American history. An active abolitionist and early member of the Republican Party, he was elected as governor of Ohio in 1855 and to the U.S. Senate in 1860, but was quickly tapped as Lincoln's secretary of the treasury, where he proposed and oversaw the formation of the national bank system. Lincoln appointed him to the Supreme Court in December 1864, where he supervised many of the postwar Reconstruction cases and the impeachment of Andrew Johnson. The building at Sixth and E streets, NW, was one of the buildings Chase occupied in Washington.

Right: The corner that once housed such a vigorous politician is now occupied by the national headquarters of the American Association of Retired Persons.

This 1880s photograph depicts the New York Avenue Presbyterian Church, established in 1803 at the junction of New York Avenue, Thirteenth Street (crossing in the foreground), and H Street (to the right of the church). Only three blocks from the White House, the church was frequently visited by many presidents, including John Quincy Adams, Andrew Jackson, Millard Fillmore, James Buchanan, Abraham Lincoln, and Andrew Johnson. The steeple shown in this photo fell in a storm in 1898 and was not replaced until 1929.

Although at first glance the modern view appears to be of the same
building, the original church was demolished by its congregation in
1950 and replaced with a church twice its size but architecturally
similar; the cornerstone was laid by Harry Truman. Its prominent
location and distinctive appearance have made it a local landmark.

This 1865 photograph depicts one of the most famous sites in American history. Built in 1863 by John Ford in what was then a disreputable part of the city, the building had been functioning as a theater for only two years when, on the night of April 14, 1865, John Wilkes Booth shot President Abraham Lincoln during a performance of *Our American Cousin*. It was the last theatrical performance at the theater until 1968. After the shooting, Lincoln was taken across the street to the Petersen House, where he died the next morning.

A year after the assassination, the federal government purchased the building and used it for office and storage space. In 1893 tragedy struck again when part of the building collapsed, killing twenty-two federal employees. The theater and the Petersen House are now operated by the National Park Service as museums memorializing the death of Lincoln, and the theater is once again used for performances.

This humble corner may be remarkable in downtown Washington in that nothing remarkable has happened on the site. The Palace Theater, one of the city's early movie theaters, is visible, as are various commercial establishments. On the other side of the block behind these buildings is the National Theater, which had recently moved into a new building on Pennsylvania Avenue (which it still occupies).

The corner is now the location of the Shops at National Place, an upscale shopping emporium just down the street from—and connected to—the National Press Building.

Many department stores opened in the downtown commercial district around the turn of the twentieth century, including the Palais Royal on G Street between Tenth and Eleventh streets, NW (which later evolved into the Woodward & Lothrop chain); Kann's; Dulin & Martin at 1215 F Street (which burned 1928); and this Hecht Company store, which was situated at the southeast corner of Seventh and F streets, NW.

This location was picketed every Thursday night and Saturday beginning in June 1951 to protest the store's denial of service to African American customers at its lunch counter. The policy was lifted in January 1952. The Hecht Company, still a thriving local chain today, moved from this location to nearby Twelfth and G streets in 1986; this building has been vacant ever since.

Located on Mt. Vernon Place at the junction of Massachusetts and New York avenues, this building was the contribution of noted American steelmaker-turned-philanthropist Andrew Carnegie. Occupying the site of the original Northern Liberty Market, it served as the central public library of Washington from 1903 to 1972. This photograph dates to 1910.

The building was used as the Carnegie Library by the University
of the District of Columbia (founded in 1976 from a merger of three
colleges) until 1998. It was then taken over as offices for construction
of the new Washington Convention Center to the immediate north,
which was completed in 2003. The building is now home to the
Historical Society of Washington, D.C.

Across the street from the U.S. Patent Office, the Merchants & Mechanics Savings Bank, located in a building built in 1865, anchored another block of commercial establishments in the Seventh Street shopping district. The men in the foreground are believed to be working on the underground electrical conduits for streetcars. The photo was taken around 1910.

The corner building has held a variety of businesses, most recently a
jewelry store that closed in the early 1990s when the MCI Center opened
across Seventh Street. Almost the entire block of Seventh Street was
vacant at the time this photo was taken. The wider area has seen a revival
as the Seventh Street Arts District, featuring galleries, museums, two
theaters (Shakespeare Theater and Fords), plus movie theaters.

In the 1100 block of Connecticut Avenue, NW, at the corner of DeSales Street, the Mayflower Hotel opened on February 18, 1925, with the inaugural ball of President Calvin Coolidge. The building was used as the residence of many important (but temporary) residents of Washington, including several vice presidents, cabinet members, Supreme Court justices, senators, and representatives.

Now on the National Register of Historic Places, the building still houses the Mayflower Hotel, as part of the Renaissance chain. A restaurant occupies the corner; down DeSales Street on the right is the Washington bureau of ABC News.

The original L'Enfant plan for Washington envisioned monuments or statues in each public square, to be erected by the states in memory of the military achievements or leaders that "were conspicuous in giving liberty and independence to this country." This photograph, from around 1890, was taken from the top of the Portland, the first apartment building in Washington, erected in 1879–80 and demolished in 1962; a modern hotel now occupies the site.

The scene has changed considerably over the years. Behind the statue can still be seen the Luther Place Memorial Church, built in 1870 as a thanksgiving to the end of the Civil War. To the left is the National City Christian Church, built in 1930 on the former home of Bishop Henry Y. Satterlee, the first Episcopal bishop of Washington (1896–1908), who planned and started the Washington National Cathedral.

Major General George H. Thomas (1816–70) was a Union general in the Civil War who earned the nickname "the Rock of Chickamauga" for his stand in the campaign for Chattanooga in September 1863. He later pursued the army of General John Hood through Tennessee, defeating them at the Battle of Nashville in December 1864. The circle at the junction of Massachusetts and Vermont avenues and M and Fourteenth streets was named in his honor on November 19, 1879, with great pageantry and a parade that lasted for two hours.

Massachusetts Avenue, which formerly passed through the circle at street level, now passes through a tunnel directly underneath the circle—a traffic-expediting strategy now common at many of the city's circles. Although the quiet peace of the vintage photograph has been shattered by bright streetlights and traffic, the statue of General George H. Thomas still stands in the center of the circle named for him.

This statue of Civil War hero Admiral Samuel Francis Du Pont (1803–65) was erected in 1884 at the circle of Massachusetts Avenue, M Street, and New Hampshire Avenue (formerly known as Pacific Circle). However, the Du Pont family, who had founded what would evolve into the Du Pont Corporation, became upset with the statue's neglect and removed the statue to the family hometown of Wilmington, Delaware, in 1920.

After the statue was removed, the Du Ponts commissioned Daniel Chester French to design this marble fountain with the allegorical figures of Sea, Stars, and Wind; it was dedicated in 1921. In a city that is not well known for spontaneity or nightlife, the Du Pont Circle neighborhood at Nineteenth and P streets, NW, is perhaps the thriving hub of Washingtonian entertainment and spectacle, the closest the city has to Times Square or Piccadilly. The only trace of its namesake, however, is an inscription on the edge of the fountain.

The Cathedral Church of St. Peter and Paul, also known as the Washington National Cathedral, was built on the site of Mt. Alban, a plot of land purchased in 1813 by Joseph Nourse, an English native who named the property after his birthplace of Mount Saint Alban in Hertfordshire. A deeply religious man, Nourse wanted his property to be used for a church, and St. Albans Episcopal Church opened in 1852. By the 1900s, plans had advanced for a Gothic cathedral on the property, which was one of the highest points in Washington. Construction began in 1907 when Theodore Roosevelt laid a foundation stone.

By 1990 the cathedral had been completed, and a dedication and consecration ceremony was held in September of that year. It now houses the tomb of Woodrow Wilson, the only president who is buried in Washington.

Established in 1851 by General Winfield Scott as the Soldiers' Home, this hospital and its sprawling grounds sit in the far northern section of the district. To the left is the Anderson Cottage, also known as Corn Riggs or the Presidents' Cottage, built by banker George Washington Riggs in 1843 and destined to be the first building of the home. It was also used as a summer home by several presidents, including Buchanan and Lincoln, in an attempt to escape the area's stifling summer heat and humidity in the days before air-conditioning.

Now known as the U.S. Soldiers' and Airmen's Home, the building has
served for over a hundred years in the role for which it was founded, as
a nursing home and hospital for military personnel who have either
been injured or have served for at least twenty years. Many additional
modern buildings also occupy the grounds.

Originally a prosperous separate entity that arose from an early 1700s tobacco-trading port on the Potomac, Georgetown formally became part of the District of Columbia in 1878. This iron bridge carried M Street (and streetcar and horsecar lines, as can be seen in this photograph) across Rock Creek just north of the junction of the creek and the Chesapeake and Ohio Canal. At the time, Rock Creek was still navigable at its lower end, and it had been used as a canal-boat staging area. This view is from the Pennsylvania Avenue bridge, which was built atop water-supply conduits that are still in place today.

The southern end of the Rock Creek and Potomac Parkway, a major commuter artery from the north, now shares the underside of the successor bridge with a considerably less navigable Rock Creek, which is just visible behind the trees on the right of the photograph.

Built in 1799 by Samuel Jackson and originally called Bellevue, this house was one of the first of many grand houses to rise on the heights of Georgetown overlooking the Potomac. The property changed hands many times over the years, in the rapid real estate speculation surrounding the founding of the federal city. During the War of 1812, it was owned by Charles Carroll, who evacuated Dolley Madison to this house when the British burned the White House in 1814.

Moved slightly from its original spot in 1915 to allow for the extension
of Q Street, the Dumbarton House at 2715 Q Street is now preserved
as a museum and headquarters of the National Society of the Colonial
Dames of America.

Seen in this photograph from the turn of the century is the sightseeing steam launch *Bartholdi* on the Potomac River west of the Aqueduct Bridge, with Georgetown University on the opposite shore. Founded in 1789, Georgetown University was the first Catholic university in the United States. The tall spires mark newly completed Healy Hall (1879). To the right on the far shore is the Washington Canoe Club, built around 1890. The trestling on the far side of the river is probably the Washington & Great Falls Electric Railway extending to Glen Echo Park via this alignment parallel to the Chesapeake & Ohio Canal.

Today a four-lane highway, an important connector between Georgetown and the northwestern suburbs, hides behind the trees on the opposite shore. Healy Hall and other, newer buildings of Georgetown University still offer a spectacular view of the Potomac River.

Built around 1765 by cabinetmaker Christopher Layman, this six-room stone house at Jefferson and M streets is regarded as the oldest (and only precolonial) building in the district. Local legend had the building as the site of George Washington's meeting with L'Enfant to plan the city, but this claim has since been refuted. The house originally served as a carpentry shop and home for Layman and his family.

In later years, the house served as a commercial
establishment, ending up as a sign-painting shop and
finally as a used-car dealer's lot and office. It is now
maintained by the National Park Service as a museum
to the modest lifestyle of everyday colonial Americans,
complete with period furnishings.

On March 30, 1791, the owners of the properties that would become the District of Columbia met with George Washington at Suter's Tavern in Georgetown. They agreed to sell their land to the government for $66.67 an acre, as well as the titles to half the building lots in the new city. Unfortunately, the exact location of this tavern has been lost to the ages. The colonial-era tavern in this photo is at Thirty-first and K streets, which some claimed was the site of Suter's Tavern, because the structure matched drawings of the building. This tavern was demolished in 1931 to make way for a city incinerator.

The site now sits in the shadow of the elevated Whitehurst Freeway, built in 1949. The incinerator closed in 1971, and as the twentieth century came to a close, the location was being developed as a $150 million luxury hotel, shopping, and twelve-screen movie theater complex. Ironically, the incinerator with its 163-foot smokestack, (visible to the left of the picture) a source of fumes and derision over the decades, became the subject of preservation efforts due to its Art Deco architecture. As part of the development scheme the base of the chimney will become a fourteen-person meeting room, while the incinerator building will host a top-floor restaurant.

In 1912, the unidentified bodies of sixty-four sailors were recovered from the wreckage of the USS *Maine*, which had exploded in Havana harbor in 1898 and thus launched the United States into the Spanish-American War. Here, the funeral procession for the sailors moves down M Street in Georgetown en route to the Aqueduct Bridge and Arlington National Cemetery. In the center of the photograph is the Key Mansion, the onetime residence of Francis Scott Key, the author of "The Star-Spangled Banner."

Built in 1802 and later operated as a museum, the Key Mansion was
unfortunately demolished in 1948–49 (despite promises to dismantle
and rebuild the structure) to make way for a ramp for the Whitehurst
Freeway. The ramp is now gone, but the adjacent Francis Scott Key
Bridge, built to replace the Aqueduct Bridge that originally carried the
Chesapeake & Ohio Canal, preserves the name.

This massive stone-arch bridge, also known as the Union Arch, was built between 1853 and 1864 by Montgomery C. Meigs as part of the water-supply aqueduct that provided Washington with water from the Cabin John Reservoir. With a clear span of 218 feet, it was the longest stone-arch span in the world for forty years. The photograph dates from about 1890.

Today the bridge carries one lane of MacArthur Boulevard over both
Cabin John Creek and the parallel Cabin John Parkway (atop the
tall wall to the left), which connect with the nearby Capital Beltway
(I-495). The formerly pastoral location of the earlier photo is now all
but inaccessible beneath the parkway and the additional water
aqueduct in the foreground.

The municipality now known as Arlington County was ceded to the federal government by Virginia in 1790, and was part of the District of Columbia until it was returned to Virginia in 1847; it was named Arlington County in 1920. This 1945 view shows the roads, ramps, and parking lots around the Pentagon still under construction.

Completed in 1943 after only two years of construction, the Pentagon, which is the headquarters for the U.S. Department of Defense, is the highest-capacity office building in the world and covers a total of thirty-four acres. It houses 23,000 military and civilian employees in five concentric buildings connected by seventeen miles of corridors.

The Arlington National Cemetery was begun in 1864 on 200 acres of property in Arlington, Virginia, belonging to the family of Robert E. Lee, which included the mansion known as Arlington House. Lee and his family abandoned the property early in the Civil War, and it was seized for nonpayment of taxes and even used as headquarters for the Union Army. The photograph shows Union soldiers on the steps of the house. Custis Lee, an heir, sued the government after the war and was awarded $150,000 for title to the land.

Arlington is now the largest and best-known of over a hundred national cemeteries, and is the final resting place for more than 245,000 servicemen and their relatives. Arlington House has been preserved and restored as the Robert E. Lee Memorial, which overlooks the graves of unknown Civil War soldiers and the grave of John F. Kennedy.

The airship *Akron* was one of the few American incursions into the short-lived aviation fad of rigid lighter-than-air aircraft. Built in its namesake Ohio city in 1931 along with its 1933 sister ship the *Macon*, it was still flying at the time of this 1933 shot despite the major changes in aircraft strategy underway at the time. The *Akron* would be lost at sea on April 4, 1933, with seventy people on board, after less than 1,700 hours of flight over twenty months. Despite the use of nonflammable helium by U.S. airships, dirigibles fell out of favor after the fatal crashes of the *Shenandoah* in 1925 and the *Macon* in 1935, as well as the burning of the German *Hindenburg* in 1937.

To the right is the east end of the Arlington Memorial Bridge, completed in 1932 to link Washington directly with Arlington National Cemetery. Beyond the Lincoln Memorial, Washington Monument, and the U.S. Capitol is the Old Post Office Tower.

Today, military jets swoop low over the location routinely on their patrols; much of the airspace around Washington, D.C., is now off-limits to civilian aircraft due to heightened security concerns.

INDEX

4th Street 32
6th Street 78–79, 82, 98–99
7th Street 36–37, 44–45, 82, 94, 106, 110–111
9th Street 96–97
10th Street 38
11th Street 42–43
12th Street 42–43, 107
13th Street 104–105
14th Street 33, 48, 50–51, 116
17th Street 58, 62, 64, 65
31st Street 132–133
Adams Building 19
Adams, John 52
American Association of Retired Persons building 99
American Institute of Architects 57
Anderson Cottage 122
Aqueduct Bridge 128, 135
Arlington County 138
Arlington Memorial Bridge 143
Arlington National Cemetery 1401–141, 143
B Street 44–45, 78–79
Bacon, Henry 72, 73
Baltimore & Ohio Railroad Station 26–27
Baltimore & Potomac Railroad Station 78, 80
Bartholdi Fountain 12–13
Bartholdi, Frédéric Auguste 12
Blair House 55
Booth, John Wilkes 102
Boston Dry Goods store 94
Botanic Garden 13
Brady, Matthew 36
Bulfinch, Charles 6, 63
Burnes, David 58
Burnes House 58
Burnham, Daniel H. 84
Burr, Aaron 51
Bush, George W. 69
C Street 26, 30–31
Cabin John Bridge 136–137
Cabin John Parkway 137
Capital Beltway 137
Capitol, The 6–7, 8–9, 10, 11, 24, 34, 40, 68, 84
Capitol Hill 26
Capitol Street 14–15, 22, 24
Carlino, John 8
Carnegie, Andrew 59, 108
Carnegie Library 109

Carroll, Charles 126
Carroll, Daniel 16
Carroll Row 14, 16–17
Casey, Thomas 68
Central Market 44, 45, 90
Central National Bank 36
Centennial Exhibition (1876) 12
Chase, Salmon P. 98–99
Chesapeake & Ohio Canal 62, 124, 135
Clinton, Bill 69
Cluss, Adolph 44, 92
Connecticut Avenue 112
Constitution Avenue 44–45, 58, 62, 78–79
Constitution Gardens 70, 73
Corcoran Gallery 64–65
Corcoran, William Wilson 64
Crawford, Thomas 11
Cret, Paul Philippe 22
D Street 32, 38
D. C. Public Library 108–109
Delaware Avenue 30–31
Desales Street 112, 113
District Building 33
Dole, Bob 69
Dolley Madison House 56–57, 126
Dumbarton House 126–127
Dupont Circle 118–119
E Street 98–99
East Grounds 14
Eastern Market 44
Ebbitt House Hotel 50
Engine Company 3 30, 31
Evans, Rudolph 74
Evening Star Building 42, 43
F Street 50–51, 96–97, 104–105, 106
FBI Building 38
Federal Triangle 35, 40, 41, 45, 47
Finley, David 93
First Street 26
Folger, Emily Jordan 22
Folger, Henry Clay 22
Folger Shakespeare Library 22–23
Ford, John 102
Ford's Theatre 102–103
Francis Scott Key Bridge 135
Franklin, Benjamin 38, 39
Freedom (statue) 11
Freedom Plaza 35
French, Daniel Chester 72, 119

G Street 107, 110–111
Garfield, James 78
Georgetown 126, 128, 129, 132, 133, 134–135
Georgetown M Street Bridge 124–125
Georgetown University 128, 129
Gilbert, Cass 24
Government Printing Office (G.P.O.) 28–29
Graves, Michael 143
Great Hall (Library of Congress) 20–21
Hadfield, George 32
Hamilton, Alexander 51, 89
Hardenbergh, Henry 49
Healy Hall 128, 129
Hecht's Department Store 106–107
Henry Bacon Drive 70
Hoban, James 52
Hotel Lombardi 77
Hutchins, Stilson 38
Independence Avenue 17, 80–81
Indiana Plaza 37
Interstate Commerce Commission buildings 39
J. Edgar Hoover Building 47
Jackson, Andrew 88
Jackson, Samuel 126
Jefferson Building 16–17, 18–19, 20–21
Jefferson Memorial 74–75, 79
Jefferson Street 130
Jefferson, Thomas 18, 74
Judiciary Square 33
K Street 132–133
Kennedy, John F. 141
Key Mansion 134, 135
King, Martin Luther 49
Layman, Christopher 130
Lee, Curtis 140
Lee House 140–141
Lee, Robert E. 140
Library of Congress 14, 15, 17, 18–19, 20–21
Lin, Maya Ying 71
Lincoln, Abraham 7, 72, 73, 102
Lincoln Memorial 68, 69, 72–73, 142–143
Lock-Keeper's House 62–63
Long Bridge 26
Luther Place Memorial Church 115
M Street 116, 118, 124, 125,

130, 134, 135
MacArthur Boulevard 137
Madison Building 17, 19
Main Post Office 34
Main Reading Room (Library of Congress) 19
Maryland Avenue 10–11, 24, 26, 82–83
Masonic Hall 96, 97
Massachusetts Avenue 108, 116, 117, 118
Mayflower Hotel 112–113
MCI Center 111
Meigs, Montgomery C. 136
Merchants and Mechanics Savings Bank building 110
Mercurio, Dan 8
Metzerott Hotel 46
Mills, Robert 66, 88
Mt. Alban 120
Mt. Vernon Place 108
Mullett, Alfred B. 61
Museum of History & Technology 14
National Air & Space Museum 81, 83
National Archives 45, 90–91
National Building Museum 29
National City Christian Church 115
National Council of Negro Women Building 37
National Gallery of Art 79, 81
National Mall 11, 69
National Museum of American Art 92–93
National Portrait Gallery 93
National Press Building 50, 51, 105
National Theater 104
National Union Insurance Co. building 96
New Hampshire Avenue 118
New Jersey Avenue 26, 31
New York Avenue 56, 65, 100, 108
New York Avenue Presbyterian Church 100–101
Nixon, Richard 70
North Lawn 53
Nourse, Joseph 120
Octagon House 56–57
Old Brick Building 24–25
Old City Hall 32–33

Old Executive Office 60–61
Old Post Office 39, 40–41, 143
Old Soldiers' Home 122–123
Old Stone House 130–131
Pacific Circle 118
Palace Theater 104
Pan American Union building 58–59
Park, Edward 7
Passaro, Tony 8
Pennsylvania Avenue 33, 34–35, 36–37, 40, 42–43, 46–47, 48, 64, 76–77, 94, 104
Pennsylvania Avenue Bridge 124
Pentagon, The 138–139
Peper, Peter 8
Petersen House 102, 103
Planet Hollywood 43
Plumbe Jr., John 6
Pollock, Isaac 76
Pope, John Russell 74, 79
Potomac Parkway 125
Potomac River 26, 62, 75, 124, 126, 128–129
Q Street 127
Quayle, Dan 61
Rayburn House Office Building 13, 83
Reagan National Airport 143
Reflecting Pool 68, 72, 73
Renwick Gallery 64–65
Renwick, James 64, 86
Rigg, George Washington 122
Riggs National Bank Building 37, 96
Rock Creek 124, 125
Roosevelt, Theodore 53, 120
Rose Garden 54
Russell Senate Office Building 31
S. Kann's Department Store 94–95
St. Florian, Friedrich 69
Saks, Andrew 94
Saks, Isodore 94
Satterlee, Henry Y. 115
Scott, Winfield 122
Shops at National Place 105
Six Buildings 76
Smith, Frederick W. 69
Smithson, James 86, 87
Smithsonian Institution Building 29, 86–87
South Carolina Avenue 44

South Lawn 54, 58
Southern Railway Building 34
Southwest/Southeast Freeway 13
Stelle, Pontius D. 16
Stephenson, Benjamin F. 37
Supreme Court Building 15, 24–25
Suters Tavern 132–133
Tayloe, Benjamin Ogle 48
Tayloe, John 56
Thomas Circle 114–115, 116–117
Thomas, George H. 116, 117
Thornton, William 56
Tidal Basin 74, 75
Treasury Building 35, 97
Truman, Harry S. 55, 101
Tucci, Joseph 8
Tweed Courthouse 38–39
U.S. Navy Memorial 94
U.S. Patent Office 92–93, 96, 110
U.S. Treasury Building 88–89
Union Arch 136–137
Union Station 27, 30, 40, 79
Union Station Plaza 27
University of the District of Columbia 109
Van Ness Mansion 58
Vermont Avenue 116
Walter, Thomas U. 7
Washington Canal 44, 62
Washington Canoe Club 128
Washington Channel 75
Washington Convention Center 109
Washington, George 14, 132
Washington Loan & Trust Co. Building 96
Washington Metro 11
Washington Monument 34, 66–67, 68, 69, 142–143
Washington National Cathedral 115, 120–121
Washington Post Building 38
Washington Union Station 84–85
White House 34, 40, 48, 52–53, 54–55, 60, 63, 126
Whitehurst Freeway 133, 135
Willard Hotel 35, 48–49, 50
Wilson, Woodrow 121
World War II Memorial 68–69